Happy Memories!
With our love and best wishes
Judith & Alan
X
November 11th 2000.

SNOWDONIA
REVISITED

SNOWDONIA REVISITED

The photography of
John Clow

Foreword by Gillian Clarke

**CREATIVE
MONOCHROME**

SNOWDONIA REVISITED
John Clow
Foreword by Gillian Clarke

Published in the UK by Creative Monochrome Ltd
20 St Peters Road, Croydon, Surrey, CR0 1HD, England

British Library Cataloguing-in-Publication Data:
A catalogue record for this book is available from
the British Library

ISBN 1 873319 22 3
First edition, 1996

Printed in England by Penshurst Press, Buckingham
House, Longfield Road, Tunbridge Wells, Kent, TN2 3EY

This book is dedicated to
the memory of my mother and father

and to
the memory of Tina

1

On Bochlwyd Buttress

ERYRI

Compelled beyond all reasoning
I am drawn again
Into this magic land;
This awesome place of shaped and timeless age;
Yet not with fear, such hallowed confines often raise,
But with a benediction born of peace
And with a warm contentment born of love.
Here, with a reverence for the power
Which man can neither conquer nor subdue,
I seek the very essence of my soul,
The reason why my spirit sings with praise,
That resonating one-ness with this world,
Yet mindful of the smallness of my state.

Gillian Clarke

'Eryri' translated, describes Snowdonia or 'the place of eagles'

Foreword

We knew each other slightly. "What are you doing here?" I asked with interest, smiling a welcome and recalling stunning photographic compositions of his. "Learning to paint," he grinned, "and you?" "I'm teaching you," I answered, unaccountably surprised that he should claim another interest aside from his camera. He looked as astonished as me. "I didn't know you painted, let alone taught," he said, and we both laughed.

So began our friendship and my admiration for this broadly gifted artist, for I learned that not only did John Clow create breathtakingly beautiful photographic prints, hewn out of time, patience and his love for Snowdonia, but that he is also a talented painter in a variety of media and a writer of lyrical poetry.

Shortly after beginning painting tuition with me, John confided that his photographic genius had reached a plateau and he had become rather disillusioned with this particular art form. All artists in whatever media will, I believe, recognise this situation. It can be quite alarming until one accepts that it provides the starting point for further growth, often in a completely new direction.

As John delved deeper into the realms of painting and the exploration of tone within colour particularly, his interest in photography reawakened and the two creative disciplines spiralled together.

Some time later, talking together about the arts in general, John asked me if I was interested in poetry. I confessed that it had been one of my passions from an early age. In his quiet unassuming way he admitted to penning the odd line and asked if I would take a look at them. It was then that I discovered another of this gentle artist's creative gifts. Obviously here was a man with something worthwhile to say about his experiences in the mountains of Snowdonia and the natural world. John not only sees beauty in nature, he is able to feel it, with a depth of emotion not given to many.

Visit John Clow in his home and you will be more than likely to hear the music of Sibelius playing while he works in his darkroom or paints in his studio, for this is another form of the arts in which John is passionately interested. "Somehow," he says, "the music of Sibelius fits how I feel about my mountains." Given that Sibelius was also heavily influenced by the power and beauty of nature, the affinity is hardly surprising. Both music and ballet touch John deeply and he has a fund of knowledge regarding both.

To walk with John Clow in the mountains of Snowdonia is truly memorable. He assails you with information: one moment you are looking skywards whilst he names a peak or points out interesting rock strata; then comes a geological lecture or detailed instructions on how to tackle a climb. The next moment you are on your hands and knees, peering at a wild flower growing in a crevice which he has spotted, and can name. Nothing escapes his eye.

But to see John at work in these mountains is quite remarkable. They are the canvas on which he labours, with the wind, the rain, mist, sunshine and shadow as his media, and with which he creates unerringly balanced compositions of unleashed elemental power. To John, photography is not merely a technical skill, but a sensation which he wishes to capture for the viewer to participate in.

Snowdonia is the catalyst between John and nature, a place where he searches for the soul of the hills and, perhaps, himself. Where he can experience the climax of a union which he finds impossible to explain, but which can happen, he says, at any time, in calm or in storm, when the spirit resonates with the natural world. It is this which comes across to us, not only in John's photography and painting, but also in his evocative poetry.

For an artist to obtain the best results from his subject matter, he must know it thoroughly. John Clow knows these mountains intimately after visiting them in all seasons and weathers for over thirty years. He escaped to them when in crisis, fled to them for comfort and retreated to them for solitude and healing, whilst they have given him unbelievable satisfaction and happiness and a never ending source of inspiration for his unforgettable work.

Gillian Clarke

Gillian Clarke is an accomplished artist and tutor in various media, who exhibits widely throughout the United Kingdom.

Introduction

"Taking in." The words floated down from on high to be swiftly followed by the slack in the climbing rope disappearing from around my feet. As the rope tightened, I shouted automatically, "That's me".

"That's me!" What am I saying and what am I doing standing on a thin rock ledge belayed to a spike of rock with space below my feet and Snowdonia spread out before me? It all seemed very familiar, but for many years my climbing rope had hung frustratingly on the banister at the foot of my stairs, and I was now sixty. John, my old climbing accomplice on so many climbs, and younger than myself, had suggested that we might climb again together and offered to lead if I would be his second.

I took no persuading, and so here I was. The legs didn't bend so easily now, but the spirit was more than willing. Caution and enjoyment were the order of the day. The thrill of climbing was undiminished, and conquering the next few feet of rock was just as exciting as always and so very immediate.

John and I had shared so many memorable climbs. One winter's day on the Cneifion Arete in a blizzard, snowflakes as large as saucers floated down silently, as numbed fingers rediscovered each handhold under the fresh covering of snow. I clearly remember reaching the top of the climb on the Gribin Ridge to be welcomed by a north-easterly wind of more than gale force. The snowflakes were not floating down now, but were being driven horizontally across the ridge beneath, in whose shelter we had been climbing. I recall quickly finding a belay, tying on and turning my back on the onslaught, hoping that John would climb the last pitch swiftly. I needn't have worried: he was up in no time and it was all that I could do to take the rope in fast enough. It was coiled in a second, in spite of the wind, and we set off down the ridge towards Ogwen Cottage as fast as we dared in the conditions.

The last long climb that we had enjoyed together was on Lliwedd during a June heatwave. The streams had dried up and all the grasses were parched yellow. I could not remember seeing the waters of Llyn Llydaw so low, but it was interesting to be able to see the glacially smoothed rocks on the eastern shore. As we neared the cliff and stopped for a rest and for a chance to study the line of the climb, John suddenly disappeared to return some considerable time later clutching a small plastic bag filled with the coolest, clearest water that you could imagine. It was nectar. I had wondered what was taking so long; he had found some water trickling over mosses in a deep, dark cleft and with his usual resourcefulness and great patience had captured half a cupful in the plastic bag. We took it in turns to have a sip until it had gone and then plodded across the brittle hillside to our chosen route.

We climbed in the shadow of this great cliff. It was delightful, enjoying the cool air and climbing lazily, resting on each belay to light our pipes and watch the smoke drift up the next pitch undisturbed by even the slightest breath of wind. We followed just as casually as the smoke, until we finally arrived at the top of the climb on the west summit. To our amazement, we saw that storm clouds were tumbling over the Nantlle hills like a huge waterfall, their progress slow, but threatening.

We ignored their presence and relaxed in the evening sunlight, watching their relentless progress out of the corner of our eyes for some considerable time, until the truth suddenly dawned upon us: our heatwave was coming to an abrupt end. We coiled the rope and hurried down to our tent, racing nature's onslaught which, we realised, was only too imminent. John cooked our dinner as the first rumbles of distant thunder sent us scurrying into the tent. Perhaps I would be excused washing-up tonight, I hoped!

A thunderstorm in the hills under canvas is an experience not to be missed. We completed our meal, and having pushed the empty crocks outside for the storm to clean, crept into our sleeping bags. Thunder reverberated around the hills and the lightning lit the landscape as if midday. Sleep would not come and we lay there marvelling at the power of nature and praying that our aluminium 'A'-frames would not be called into use as lightning arrestors.

We didn't need a plastic bag to catch the water now. The rain came down in sheets, drumming on our sagging flysheet, but it was made of stern stuff and resisted the torrent. We were dry in our man-made cavern, but humbled by the power being unleashed all around and the majesty of the storm. Finally, it ebbed away like the outgoing tide, and in the deepening silence, sleep drifted into the tent. Tomorrow would bring another adventure.

I felt a gentle tug on the rope, followed by a more urgent one, suggesting that I make a move. I quickly untied my belay. "Climbing", I shouted and started up the steep slab above. When I neared the top of the pitch, I could see John's feet dangling in space: he had obviously found a comfortable perch upon which to belay and as I neared he peered down, grinning from ear to ear. "Daydreaming?" he enquired. Nothing had changed. We were back on the rocks. Father Time had marched on and my limbs were a little stiffer, but the hills were the same.

Inevitably, the karabiner has given way to the camera and I now share the wild cwms with the wind and rain, with the fleeting sunlight and transparent mists which remodel each day that wonderful landscape. They are my mountains of longing; when I am not there my only wish is to return, for they have been my friends for so long.

I treasure my yesterdays
they have made today.
Today is all my yesterdays.

John Clow

When I glance upstream
I sense the mountains,
brooding there,
waiting.

2
Winter, Afon Nanmor

3
Winter, Afon Nanmor

4
February morning, Cwm Idwal

5

Lliwedd across Llyn Teyrn

6
Towards Lliwedd and Gallt y Wenallt

7

Yr Wyddfa across Llyn Llydaw

THE TRAETH MISTS

It was a fine October morning. I left Capel Curig and drove past a Llynau Mymbyr partially hidden by writhing mist, which thickened by the minute until visibility was only a few yards.

I parked the car and decided to climb the hillside towards the Glyders to see if I could get above the blanket of cloud. I struggled up through golden-tipped bracken, pale grasses heavy with moisture, and twisted hawthorns bearing winter fruit.

Suddenly the mist thinned, revealing high above a canopy of blue and below me a sea of cloud. I was standing above Dyffryn, the mountain sheep farm of which Thomas Firbank wrote in his best-selling novel, *I Bought a Mountain*.

Across the valley, Moel Siabod floated distant and elegant, whilst the head of the valley framed the twin summits of Lliwedd, now reflecting the first rays of the morning sun. The mist below heaved and sighed, as if unsure of what to do as the rising sun warmed the landscape.

The mist decided to clear and so I returned to the car and made my way to the head of the Gwynant Valley, which was still partially hidden by the vapours billowing below. As the veil was drawn almost imperceptibly aside, Yr Aran appeared and, as time passed, the autumnal colours of the woodland below grew in intensity to provide a vista of unparalleled charm.

The mists, called the 'Traeth Mists' are, according to local legend, nature's attempt to reclaim the land which man has won from the sea at Traeth Mawr. These ephemeral and transient mists are formed – usually in spring or autumn – by warm, moist air from the sea flowing up the Gwynant Valley to become trapped in the colder air at the head of the cwm.

8
Morning mists, Dyffryn

9

Gwynant Valley and the Traeth Mists

10
Dawn mists, Dyffryn

11
Sunlight and mist, Gwynant Valley

12
Sunlight and mist, Gwynant Valley

IN MIRRORED DEPTHS

Maytime sun
and lofty clouds
in mirrored depths.

Beneath the surface,
hiding there
with loneliness.

And then the wind
so silently
hides all.

13
Sunlight and shade, Llyn Padarn

14
Maytime reflections, Llyn Padarn

15
Across Llyn Padarn

16
Reflections, Llyn Padarn

17
almost –
just loneliness
remains

TO TRYFAN

Evening's cloak
hangs sombre grey,
but slowly
the dark veil
is drawn aside.

Soft sunlight
filters through
transparent mists,
to slip behind
the darkening peaks.

A quietness, more impressive
than any sound,
now holds a landscape
surrendering to
the depths of night.

LAST LIGHT ON TRYFAN

A wet and windy March day was coming to an end. Damp stratus clouds shrouded the hills as I parked the car in the Ogwen Valley. Leaving the engine running to provide comfort against the bitterly cold wind which was blowing up the valley, I settled down to read and then became aware of a faint light in the sky above, where Tryfan usually dominated the vista to the west.

Was I dreaming? I knew that the evening sun would be in that direction – could it be clear? I jumped out of the car in an instant, grabbed camera and tripod and set off up the mountain-side to where I knew I would get a clear view of Tryfan, should I be that lucky. I set the camera on the tripod and went through my exposure ritual with the spotmeter. It was cold, very cold, and in my haste I had left my duvet in the car. There was no time to worry, so I calculated the exposure, set the camera and withdrew the dark-slide. The light in the sky promptly disappeared.

I waited and waited, but the gloom and cold increased as my resolve waned. I returned, defeated, to the car and warmth, to imagine what might have been. Revelling in the comfort, I dozed off, or did I? I thought I sensed a light in the sky over Tryfan beckoning: was the evening sun really there? I wiped the misty window. It wasn't a dream.

I shot out of the car and up the hillside, setting up the camera in a trice. I had time to notice that it was still very cold, as I had left the duvet behind yet again. I forgot my numbed fingers as the muted light in the west grew in strength and Tryfan was slowly reincarnated from its shroud, shreds of which were drawn this way and that, writhing around the east face, finally to disappear in the evening sky. Eventually the silhouette of Tryfan stood out starkly whilst a river of mist flowed gently down from the Glyders, beneath the slope of Heather Terrace and into the waiting valley.

The darkness deepened and when I could no longer see Adam and Eve gracing the central buttress of Tryfan's summit, I made my way downhill in the stillness, whilst Tryfan was swallowed into the depths of another winter night.

18 - 20
Towards Tryfan

21
Towards Tryfan

22
Tryfan and Bristly Ridge

ROCK AND SNOW

Rock and snow,
mists and fleeting sunlight;
a biting wind that from the east arrives
to stir the clouds,
that race in turmoil
midst Eryri's soaring peaks.

23
Crib Goch and Crib y Ddysgl

24
Crib Goch and Crib y Ddysgl

25
Crib Goch and Lliwedd

26
Bryn Du

27
Llyn Gwynant

28
Crib Goch

29
Towards Lliwedd

30
In Cwm Padrig

31
In Cwm Padrig

32
Ffynnon Lloer

33
Ffynnon Lloer

34
Tryfan

35
Tryfan

36
Y Garn

WATER

Hear water
sliding between dark rocks.
See dappled sunlight
caressing its surface.

Listen to water
sparkling and foaming,
spilling and dancing
down distant falls.

Watch how water,
angry now, roaring,
leaps down the hillside
after the storm.

See icy water
locked still and sombre,
held by white silence.
Awaiting the spring.

37
Afon Cwm Llan

38
Afon Cwm Llan

39
Afon Cwm Llan

40
Afon Cwm Llan

41
Afon Cwm Llan

42
Afon Cwm Llan

43
Afon Cwm Llan

44
Afon Cwm Llan

above: 45
Afon Idwal

opposite: 46; 47
Cwm Idwal; Carneddau

WHEN IN DOUBT, GO TO OGWEN

It was 7.30 as I drove down to Llyn Padarn to check on the early morning light. A strong wind was blowing and clouds were scudding across the hilltops. The choppy surface of the lake was veiled in grey. I turned the car and drove back up past Deiniolen over the high road and back to Mynydd Llandegai. 'When in doubt go to Ogwen' is my golden rule, so I dropped down the steep winding road, past the lovely church of St Ann, to join the A5 road near the entrance to Penrhyn quarry. It was still overcast as I drove up the Nant Ffrancon. As I neared Ogwen, I could see mist being blown out right over the road. I suddenly realised that it wasn't mist at all, but spray, and that it could only have come from Cwm Idwal.

I had tried on many occasions to capture an image of very high winds peeling off the surface of a lake and throwing it into the air. I had always failed, but perhaps I was far enough up the learning curve now. I had to try. I hurriedly left the car in a deserted car park at Ogwen Cottage, threw on an anorak and rucksack, and hurried up through the narrow quarry that leads to Cwm Idwal. I could not believe it. There was not a breath of wind!

'Have I been thwarted again?' I asked myself. I need not have worried, for as I climbed out of the shelter of the narrow passageway and onto the hillside, I was almost bowled over by a gust of wind. I struggled on, bent double against the onslaught, and when eventually I topped the rise and could see Llyn Idwal, I could hardly believe my eyes. The usually placid waters were foaming, and with each gust of wind the maelstrom was flung into the air to greet my advance. I was soon quite damp and realised that, in my excitement, I had left my waterproofs in my rucksack and that in this wind it would be extremely difficult, if not impossible, to put them on. The more urgent question was: could I photograph the drama in the Cwm. I had tried before and failed in less demanding circumstances. Nothing is more confusing than a strong wind: each simple task becomes a problem.

During the short lulls I managed to set up the tripod and get a camera onto it – not daring to let go. My rucksack, relieved of this weight, was inclined to join forces with the wind and attempt to depart over the hill behind me. I solved this problem by wrapping one of the bag's shoulder straps around my ankle. When the ferocious blasts arrived, laden with soaking spray, I had to hang on to and shield the camera at the same time. There was no-one around to hear me admonishing the wind, but even had there been anyone, I doubt they could have heard a word against the howling gale.

Keeping the lens clear of moisture was the most urgent and frustrating problem. I always carry two handkerchiefs, one for my nose and one for my camera, but in the total confusion they both became equally wet. I did my best and lived in hope that the lens was clear enough to record something. I stuck at it for two hours until the wind's strength died a little. Changing the rolls of film had been a nightmare, but to be there to witness the drama and to experience the force of the wind and watch the spray flung into the air and to see the waves racing across the llyn towards me was unforgettable.

When I turned to go, I grabbed the camera, tripod and rucksack, and somehow we were carried effortlessly uphill in total disarray and then down to seek the shelter of the quarry. Once there, I restored some semblance of order by pushing all my gear into the rucksack, whilst the wind roared its disapproval overhead. The tea shop at Ogwen was open by now and I downed steaming coffee to the friendly enquiry, "You haven't been on the hill, surely?".

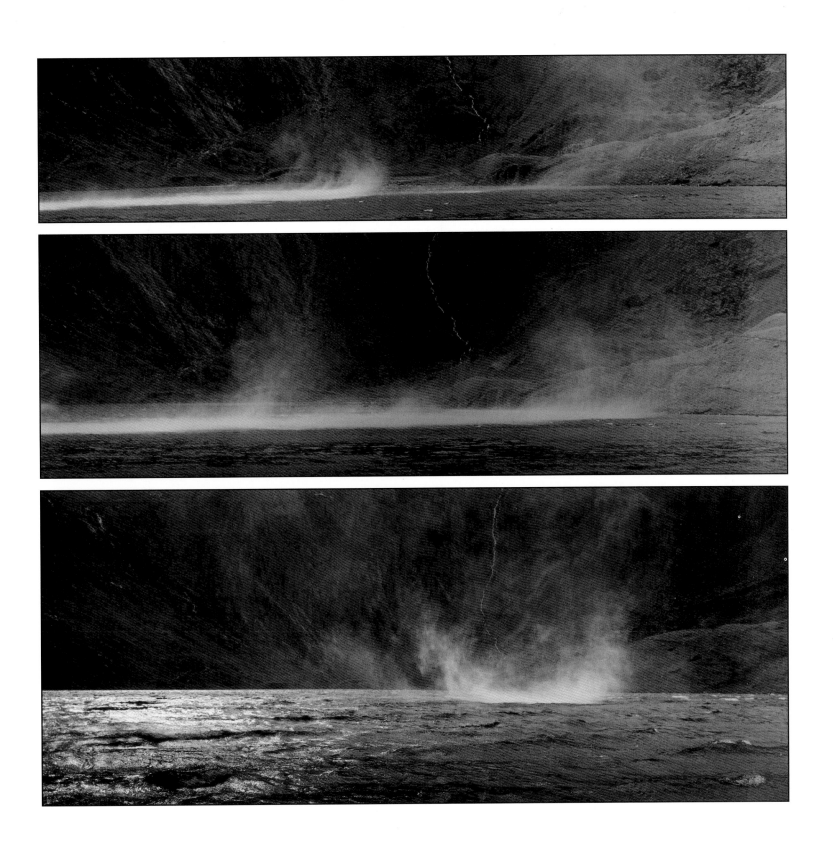

48 - 50
Cwm Idwal

IDWAL IS ANGRY TODAY

Idwal is angry today.
The warrior Wind
has trespassed his domain.
He explodes in anger
to drive the usurper out.

Wave chases wave
across the forlorn waters.
The wind tears their crests,
sending them scurrying
furiously away.

The battle ebbs and flows
whilst the patient cwm
waits until,
the warrior's fury spent,
peace will return to Idwal.

opposite: 51 - 52
Cwm Idwal

No implements of man
have carved these rocks,
but wind and water
and the hand of time.

53
Cwm-y-ffynnon

54
Afon Lloer

55
Trearddur Bay

56

Glyder Fawr and Glyder Fach

Glyder Fawr and Glyder Fach

58
Yr Aryg

59
Garnedd Uchaf

60
Afon Glaslyn

61

Castell y Gwynt

BLOW WIND

Blow wind,
carry your fragile tresses
over waiting hills;
nestle in lone cwms
and touch the dark waters
with Merlin's wand.

Fly on,
up steepening ramparts
of rock aretes and spires;
deep gullies cleft
guiding your upward path
to greet the heavens.

62
Lliwedd and Llyn Llydaw

63 - 65
Lliwedd and Llyn Llydaw

PALE DAWN

Pale dawn,
peace that dwells upon the valley floor.
Faint mist and muted light
that hold the hills subdued,
who guard the silence of the morn'.

A gentle wind,
aroused by dawn's increasing warmth,
drifts through the hillside birches.
Branches quiver with the wind's embrace
and welcome yet another day.

66

Nant Ffrancon

WATERS FALLING

Waters falling, ghost-like
through the mist;
silent, distant.
A blessing pouring
onto cold grey rocks,
bringing life and promise;
a promise of tomorrow.

67
Cwm Dyli

68
Cwm Dyli

69
Llyn Glaslyn

ASCENT OF CARNEDD DAFYDD

The mists are down to the foot of the bed
and stillness holds the land.
The lofty peaks in silence rise,
their summits in the clouds.

I must obey that call
to share their peace on high,
and climb above the land of men
to where the giants sleep.

Through ghostly woodland,
ash and birch stand sombre by,
their branches hanging
with the morning dew.

Out onto grassy banks,
short cropped,
where the dark forms of gorse
share passage with the sheep.

A warm transparent glow appears
through the moist air,
a patchwork quilt of rushes
thriving there to shape my path.

The hillside steepens,
fescue and matt grass
adorn the mountainside
before the rocky wastes above.

From each dim viewpoint on I go
past scattered screes,
to frost heaved soils
so gentle underfoot.

The final ramparts I survey,
grey blocks of mountain
jumbled high through the dark mist.
"Dafydd, are you sleeping there?"

In silence I approach the summit cairn,
to sit in quiet contemplation
on the welcoming rocks
and feel the still benevolence enfold.

Where else on earth
can man such solace find?
For nature shares her gifts alone
with those that love her ways.

SOMEWHERE

The path goes on,
I can see it in the distance
twisting in and out of lonely cwms.
It appears to go on for ever,
but it must end
somewhere.

Up past a singing stream
which rushes downhill, haphazard, happy,
frolicking and foaming midst rounded rocks
and fresh green ferns
carrying the mountains away,
somewhere.

Clouds are threatening, grey and ominous
and the wind freshens.
Sunlight sweeps across the landscape
and is gone beyond a distant ridge
to cheer another valley,
somewhere.

The damp air swirls around
brimming with moisture,
suspended in space,
carried this way and that,
enriching all as it alights
somewhere.

The squall departs as quickly as it came.
The delicate grasses now
parabolas of tiny water droplets,
glisten in the brightening scene,
the wind departing too,
somewhere.

Each raindrop trembling,
splintering the sunlight as if cut glass,
sparkling crystal.
The colours of the rainbow held
within each transparent globe,
somewhere.

The hillside glows,
an oasis of soft light,
stark contrast with the now distant gloom
that brought the rain
then rainbows in its wake, from
somewhere.

My path continues.
There is no end, just a promise
of tomorrow, another beginning.
Life's silver lining
accompanying each passing storm,
somewhere.

ON MOEL HEBOG

The heavens were the proscenium arch,
the stage and lighting set.
A backloth of subtle greys
encircled my world.

Wherever I looked
between sky and earth below,
awesome shapes floated in space
perfect in line and form.

Yr Wyddfa there
casting a brief glance,
a veil of white gossamer
draping those mighty flanks.

A gentle wind the only voice
whispering between the summit rocks.
There was no distance, no time,
simply an all-enveloping feeling of calm.

REMEMBER

Remember the blue distance, remember,
where flotillas of white galleons set their sails;
where are they journeying?
Billowing cumulus in lines so straight
between the earth and sky, voyaging afar.

Writhing patterns of Menai at low tide
and Anglesey, a chequered land of white and green,
spread forth to melt with distant, hazy seas.
The Rivals and Great Orme
floating there in the uncertainty of time.

Above the arching pale green moorland stand
Yr Elen and Llywelyn proudly there,
gaunt greys and browns towering beneath a sapphire sky.
Y Garn and Elidir a distant blue.
Remember that you stood on Foel Fras?

Remember too the skylark above your downward path,
its welcoming song so shrill and clear,
wild ponies grazing as you made your homeward way.
Remember too the ending of the day,
the mellow landscape and the evening breeze.

Beyond the shimmering waters of the bay,
the shafts of gold were deepening to a crimson glow,
the evening sun slipped slowly out of sight.
Cool rivers of night flooded into valley depths,
and stillness settled o'er the darkening land. Remember?

(written on Foel Fras)

TO SNOWDONIA

Freedom there
beneath that
canopy of time;
vast vistas,
rolling hills
and rocky summits.

Wind that
calls from afar,
carries one's spirit
to pastures new
of untold beauty
and of peace.

74
The northern hills of Snowdonia
from the high ground to the east of the Conway Valley

75
Elidir Fawr and Foel Goch, September
seen from the Carnedds

76
Towards Moel Siabod

77
Moel Elio

78
Moorland near Bera Mawr, Carneddau

85
Welsh ponies on the hillside below the High Carneddau

86
Black headed gulls nesting in Cwm Glas

87
Early morning mist, Tryfan

88

Tryfan across the waters of Llyn Clyd Bach